A PUG'S
GUIDE TO
Dating

A PUG'S
GUIDE TO
Dating

GEMMA CORRELL

DOG 'n' BONE

Published in 2013 by Dog 'n' Bone Books
An imprint of Ryland Peters & Small Ltd

20–21 Jockey's Fields
London WC1R 4BW

519 Broadway, 5th Floor
New York, NY 10012

www.rylandpeters.com

10 9 8 7 6 5 4

A CIP catalog record for this book is available from
the Library of Congress and the British Library.

ISBN: 978 1 909313 10 1

Printed in China

Editor: Pete Jorgensen
Designer: Jerry Goldie
Illustration: Gemma Correll

For digital editions, visit www.cicobooks.com/apps.php

CONTENTS

INTRODUCTION

Wrinkly of face and fragrant of backside, the pug is one of nature's most romantic creations. A twenty-pound, wheezing, farting Lothario with an undeniably magnetic allure that no creature—of the canine persuasion or otherwise—can resist.

Nonetheless, even for these naturally amorous and handsome creatures, the world of love can be a daunting and confusing place; a minefield of potential mistakes and misjudgments. The pug who abides, as most do, by the laws of etiquette and decorum that govern his kind, will understand the need to tread carefully, to study and strive to comprehend the conventions that govern the world of curly-tailed courting.

To the casual observer, it may appear that the pug, possessed as he is with natural charm and charisma, dashing good looks, and an infinite repertoire of alluring snorty noises, finds it easy to attract any number of admirers. And indeed, this is fundamentally the case—most creatures of any intelligence, upon meeting him, are immediately smitten.

However, even the most confident pug may require guidance in the sometimes bewildering world of modern dating. For example, he must learn how to present himself in a personal ad or at a speed-dating event, or he must determine how to find the most suitable and romantic location for a first date.

Essentially, he must become a dedicated scholar in the art of love, pondering upon the very fundamentals of flirtation, seeking to master the basic principles of poetry, song, and dance, and conquering the elementary techniques of kissing and snuggling.

Once comfortably ensconced in a relationship, the pug must endeavor to keep the "flame" of love alive, ensuring that the erstwhile heady days of puppy love, although in the past, are never forgotten. He must never forget a special occasion such as an anniversary or canceled veterinary appointment, ensuring that he lavishes gifts and passionate, intense kisses upon his sweetheart at every opportunity.

REMEMBER TO STOP AND SMELL THE ROSES.
IF NECESSARY, YOU SHOULD ALSO PEE ON THEM.

Sadly, the pug's unconditionally loving and devoted temperament can work against him in the event of a break-up. He, sensitive creature that he is, may find himself quite undone by the painful heartbreak that so often accompanies a separation. One hesitates to label the pug with the hyperbolic terms "neurotic" or "obsessive" but he does seem to take all forms of separation, whether from his human, his sweetheart, or even from a favorite toy, particularly badly. It is imperative, therefore, that he learns to cope with rejection and heartache in a useful and healthy manner.

The love of a pug is faithful and unwavering. He is a devoted partner; a generous and caring paramour with a face full of wrinkles and a heart of gold. As the old saying goes...

"To know a pug is to love him."

Chapter 1

BREAKING THE ICE

FIRST IMPRESSIONS

First impressions count. Take care to maintain a memorably fragrant derrière at all times. After all, you never know whom you might be lucky enough to bump into!

PICK-UP LINES

Come here often?

You must be tired... you've been running through my mind all day.

Did you just roll in fox poop or is that your natural aroma?

Hey baby, I like your wrinkles.

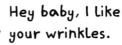

SPEED DATING

Attending a speed-dating event is a great,
fun way to meet other lonely hearts.

CHANCE ENCOUNTERS

Romance might not be the first thing on your mind when visiting the vet (it's more likely to be a desperate urge to pee on the examination table) but love can blossom in the most unexpected places...

HOW TO TELL IF SHE LIKES YOU

A pug shows affection quite readily, so it can be difficult to differentiate between a naturally friendly demeanor and real affection.

Watch out for these signs that she wants to be more than "just friends"...

She mirrors your body language...

I AVERAGE 250 LICKS PER MINUTE.

She shows off in front of you...

She tries the old "Damsel in Distress" act...

She brings you gifts...

ASKING HER OUT

Choose your moment and your location wisely. Pick a time and a place where she is relaxed and comfortable, like just after a good poop in the grumpy next-door neighbor's front garden.

REMAIN POSITIVE

Dont be intimidated! Remember, you may be small but you are perfectly formed.

Your potential partner will almost certainly say "yes." Who can resist a face like that?

REJECTION

Don't be disheartened if she says "no"—
it's her loss.

However, you should ham it up as much as
possible in order to secure more sympathetic
belly rubs, and possibly extra kibble, from
your human.

Sigh repeatedly, squeeze yourself into tight
spaces, and generally mope around looking
pathetic. Humans are weak. They will fall
for it.

PERSONAL ADS

HAMSTER WITH GSOH seeks stimulating company for weekends in the wheel, carrot nibbling, and other activities. Ginger short-haired rabbit enjoys eating lettuce. Must be fit and no one over 4 months. Box No. 445677

CAT (f) with sociopathic tendencies seeks tom cat for chair scratching and tail chasing during the day. Must be spayed and have own flea collar.

FAWN, NEUTERED PUG (3)
With double-curled tail seeks
easy going lady for ear licking
and maybe more. Must enjoy
bacon, barking at inanimate
objects, and cuddles on the sofa
GSOH, NS, SWM, PUG
Box No. 652732

EXOTIC PARROT with authority issues, GSOH seeks similar. Must enjoy incessant chatter and have own cage. NS, NSFW, DOX No. 344277

WHIPPET, F, 21 (in dog years) looking for true love. ALL breeds considered. Athletic build, short attention span. Must like running and chasing cats.

If you are having trouble finding a suitable partner using the conventional route, you might like to try online dating, or you could place a personal ad in the newspaper.

FINDING MR. OR MRS. RIGHT

Love knows no size, color, or breed.

Although the object of your affection may not always share this philosophy.

First Date

Hurrah! Your crush has agreed to a rendezvous. But where to go? Here are some ideas:

A romantic stroll presents the perfect opportunity for you to impress your sweetheart with your worldly knowledge...

I JUST LOVE PASTRIES

While a visit to a local café allows you to get to know each other in a comfortable environment, with the added bonus of a floor full of crumbs on which to nibble.

If you are culture vultures, you may both enjoy a visit to a gallery or for hip young urbanites a street art exhibition.

There are those who say that you should never sleep together on the first date. But we say—do whatever makes you happy!

GROOMING

Of course, you'll want to look—and smell—your very best for your first date.

PEE PEE
pour carlin

Exclusively for pugs

Dead
PARFUM
squirrel

With hints of badger

EAU
–de–
FOX POO

Earthy and bright

TOILET
WATER
NO. 1

A classic

WHAT TO WEAR

A harness and leash are perfectly appropriate
first-date attire, but if you really want to
make an impression, ask your human to choose
an outfit for you.

Something understated and subtle, yet
undeniably sexy—like a lobster costume
or a giant banana suit—should do the trick.

ROMANTIC KEEPSAKES

When you visit your sweetheart at home, be sure to leave a memento for her to remember you by. Perhaps a generous sprinkling of fur atop a contrasting-colored sofa...

A selection of decorative paw prints across a freshly mopped floor...

BEAUTIFUL!

Or simply your own delightfully pungent natural scent.

LOOKING YOUR BEST

An enlightened pug knows how to make the best of whatever he has to work with.

Chapter 3

ROMANCE

Poetry

Nothing is more romantic than poetry.
Except maybe a box of heart—shaped meaty
treats (hint hint).

OH, BLACK IS THE COLOR
OF MY TRUE LOVE'S COAT,
HER FACE SO FLAT AND HER
WRINKLY THROAT.
THE BIGGEST EYES
AND THE SCRATCHIEST PAWS
I LOVE THE GROUND ON
WHICH SHE SNORES.

ROSED ARE RED,
VIOLETS ARE BLUE.
IF I SNIFF YOUR BUM,
WILL YOU SNIFF
MY BUM TOO?

MY LOVE FOR YOU IS LIKE MY MORNING PEE;
IT GOES ON AND ON AND ON... AND ON.

MY LOVE FOR YOU IS LIKE A SNEEZE;
SLOPPY, WET, AND IN YOUR FACE.

MY LOVE FOR YOU IS LIKE
A SQUEAKY TOY;
IT DRIVES ME CRAZY.

MY LOVE FOR YOU IS LIKE
A BOWL FULL OF KIBBLE;
DELICIOUS AND... MMMM...
WAIT, WHAT WAS I
TALKING ABOUT?

DANCE

The art of dance is sensual and passionate.
Here are a few moves that you might like
to try...

THE DANCE OF THE FLYING PILLOWS

LE GRAND JETÉ (AUX DEUX HUNGRY PUGS)

THE BOOTY WIGGLE

THE POOPY KICKIN' JIVE

THE CARPET SURF BOOGIE

THE FART 'N' TWIST

THE TAIL CHASIN' REEL

THE DINNERTIME
JITTERBUG

KISSING

It's no secret that we pugs love to kiss. The most popular smooching style is of course the traditional, vigorous, and incessant "pug lick," which is used to show affection toward another creature, whether animal, human (familiar or strange), or inanimate object.

Here are some other kissing styles that are favored among pug—kind...

ESKIMO KISS

FRENCH KISS

EAR NIBBLES

NECKING

THREE—WAY KISS

STARGAZING

The night sky is the window
to the universe. Spend a romantic
evening stargazing with your beloved.
Look out for famous constellations
like CANIS MINOR (the little dog) and
CATTUS STUPIDUS (the stupid cat).

SERENADING

Pugs are known to possess beautiful singing voices. Make the most of this natural talent by performing a heartfelt, sentimental composition extolling the many virtues of your inamorata— a cappella, of course.

CHAPTER 4

SPECIAL OCCASIONS

VALENTINE'S DAY

On Valentine's Day, it is traditional for sweethearts to exchange gifts.

Here are a few great gift ideas:

TREAT SELECTION BOX

SEXY LINGERIE (WORN)*

BOUQUET OF
USED TISSUES

TEDDY BEAR*

*for chewing purposes

A Romantic Weekend

Spend some quality time together. Why not treat yourself and your partner to some fancy spa treatments, expertly administered by your personal human—assistant?

AYURVEDIC BELLY MASSAGE

WET DISHTOWEL BODY WRAP
(SUMMER SPECIAL)

DETOXING FULL–BODY BRUSH

KIBBLE AND WET FOOD FACIAL

(may be accompanied by a push–the–bowl–around–the–floor workout)

We recommend that you avoid the pedicure.

A Romantic Dinner

Celebrate special occasions, like anniversaries or canceled veterinary appointments, with a romantic dinner in a suitably enchanting location.

Try the kitchen floor or the back yard for a delightful al fresco tête-à-tête.

MENU SUGGESTIONS

APPETIZERS

Medallions of cat poop nestled on a bed of crispy ryegrass.

Assortment of amuse-bouches.

ENTRÉES

Pan-fried tissues in an organic peanut butter jus.

Artisan underwear atop a purée of pinecones.

DESSERTS

Hamster droppings in a decadent vomit compote.

TO DRINK...

"Yellow Snow" margarita.

Toilet water sorbet served in a French-style tennis ball.

Our special "Puddle Water" martini.

I ♥ MY PUG

Gourmet "Day-Old" coffee.

Anniversaries

It is a custom among pugs and other dogs to celebrate anniversaries with gifts that symbolize the number of (dog) years that they have been together.

1 YEAR

TURKEY & RICE

7 YEARS

KIBBLE

14 YEARS

BISCUITS

21 YEARS

PEANUT BUTTER

28 YEARS

BONE

35 YEARS

BACON

Also commonly performed during anniversary celebrations is the ancient pug tradition of "THE LICKING OF THE FLOOR."

This ritual should always be undertaken with purpose and dedication. A floor—licking ceremony can last anywhere between a couple of minutes to several hours.

It may be performed on any surface, including carpet, linoleum, and concrete.

Another popular anniversary custom is the "Dinnertime Observance," whereupon the happy pug couple maintain a thrice-daily vigil underneath the hallowed "table of the humans," waiting in anticipation for sacred "tidbits" to fall.

This ritual has deep significance. The table symbolizes life, the humans represent fate, and the crumbs are symbolic of everlasting love.

Fighting over the crumbs is generally thought to be inauspicious.

PET NAMES

Once a couple have celebrated their first anniversary together, they will no doubt have developed pet names for each other. These monikers are terms of endearment used by a romantically involved couple, often inspired by a physical characteristic or personality trait.

LICKLICK

SNORTFACE MCDRIBBLE

FATBOY

MR WRINKLES

LITTLE PIRATE

GRUMPS

**TOOTHY
O'WORMFACE**

SIR STINKSALOT

WONKY

CHAPTER 5

RELATIONSHIPS

LOVE IS...

Patience and understanding...

LOVE IS...

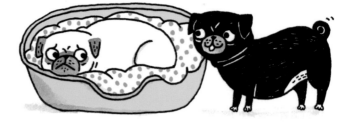

all about...

two people...

PREPARED TO COMPROMISE...

LOVE IS...

Feeling comfortable and relaxed together...

And accepting each other, flaws and all.

Love is unconditional.

KEEPING THE ROMANCE ALIVE

The couple that...

CHIN RESTS
TOGETHER

SUNBATHES
TOGETHER

HEAD TILTS
TOGETHER

... stays together.

SHOWING YOU CARE

Make sure you let your loved one know how much they mean to you.

Say "I love you" every day in your own special way. (A lingering wet lick will almost certainly also be appreciated.)

DON'T GET STUCK IN A RUT

When you first get together, it's all very exciting and new. After a while, though, you may find yourself in such a familiar routine that you end up taking each other for granted. Avoid this by keeping things exciting.

Try some new positions in bed, such as...

THE PILLOW LICKER

THE PILLOW FARTER

Your human will appreciate these too.

AFFAIRS

Pugs are generally faithful creatures, but a young, naive pug may be tempted to snuggle with someone besides his significant other.

It's not the end of the world, unless you are tempted to snuggle the hamster...

Then it might be (for him anyway).

Chapter 6
BREAKUPS

Niggles

In a long-term relationship, you may find that some things begin to annoy you about your partner.

WHY DOES SHE HAVE TO BE SUCH A DRAMA QUEEN?

Every relationship has its ups and downs.

THE END IS NIGH

Sadly, some relationships must come to an end, and a breakup can be utterly devastating for the sensitive pug.

Symptoms of Heartbreak

You might find that you have problems eating.

Your sleeping patterns may become irregular.

You may even suffer from physical symptoms such as gastrointestinal upsets.

GETTING OVER IT

A breakup is tough, but you can get through it. You are a pug! Master of the universe! King of the curly tails! You can do anything!

You can lick your own nose, for goodness sake.

Remember to stay active.
(Never neglect your thrice daily "Pug Run.")

Don't forget to look after yourself.

Take time out to reflect.

LETTING IT OUT

Try some stress—relieving exercises, such as barking at the TV. (This is particularly effective when performed during your human's favorite TV shows.)

SOCIALIZING

Spending some quality time with your best
friends will soon help you forget about things.

Je Ne Regrette Rien

Even if a love affair ends badly (you were a pug, she was a Labradoodle... the rest is history...), don't look back with sadness or regrets.

Leave the past behind you, like a particularly stinky fart, and move on.

The future awaits! And it's bacon flavored.

HOPE

Never forget, there are plenty more dogs in the park and someone special out there for every pug.

A Final Word

A wise pug once said,

All you need is love,
Kibble,
and a de-worming tablet
every three to six months.

Acknowledgments

Thank you Anthony, my partner in life, studio, and stupid in-jokes (Baka-ahh).

Thanks Team Little Red Roaster and Lucy (I'm still cross with you, though) and to all my friends and family for putting up with, nay, actively encouraging my ridiculous pug obsession.

Thank you to everyone at Dog 'n' Bone and Cico, especially Pete Jorgensen and, of course, one big belly rubbing thank you to my muses Mr. Pickles and Bella for never ceasing to amuse and inspire me.